A CHARLIE AND BANDIT ADVENTURE

# AN EGYPTIAN ESCAPE

ADVENTURE BY

## K.A. GERRARD

DRAWN BY

## EMMA DODD

templar publishing

Hi, I'm Charlie and this is my dog, Bandit.

Our first adventure, to ancient Rome, all started when a huge sinkhole appeared in our back garden.

Turns out that it can take you back in time!

After falling down it once, we decided that we'd **NEVER** make that mistake again...

# AN EGYPTIAN ESCAPE

For Kelly, E.D. x
For Peter with love, K.A.G.

A Templar Book
First published in the UK in 2012 by Templar Publishing,
an imprint of The Templar Company Limited,
The Granary, North Street, Dorking, Surrey, RH4 1DN
www.templarco.co.uk

Text copyright © 2012 by Kelly Gerrard
Illustration copyright © 2012 by Emma Dodd

First edition

ISBN 978-1-84877-628-9

Edited by Libby Hamilton

Printed in Hong Kong

# CHAPTER 4: I WANT MY MUMMY

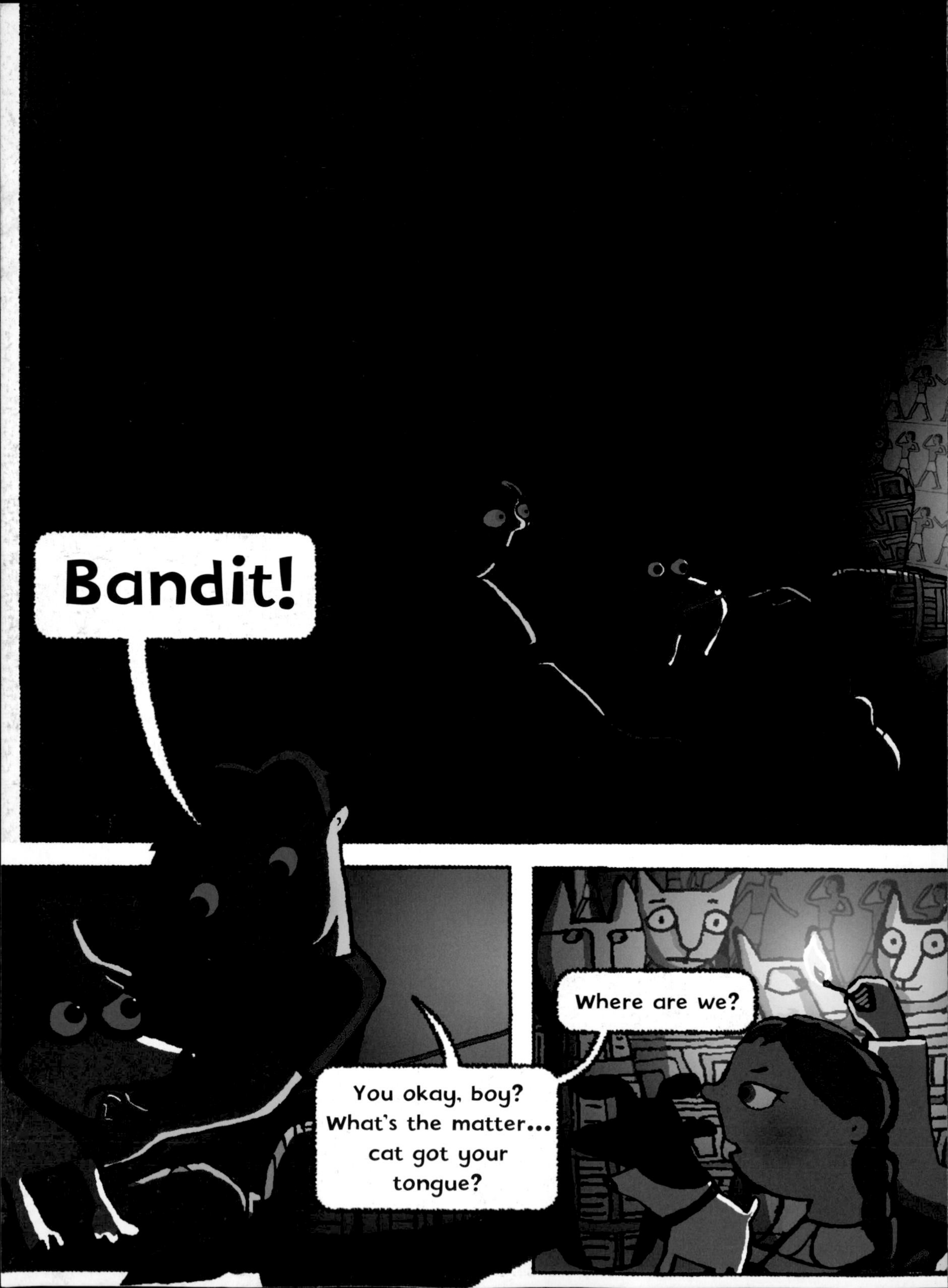

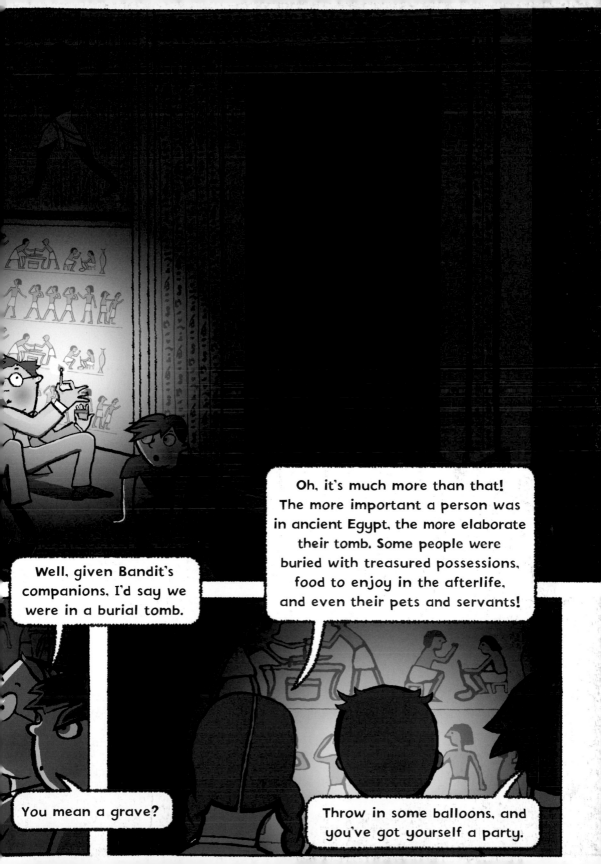

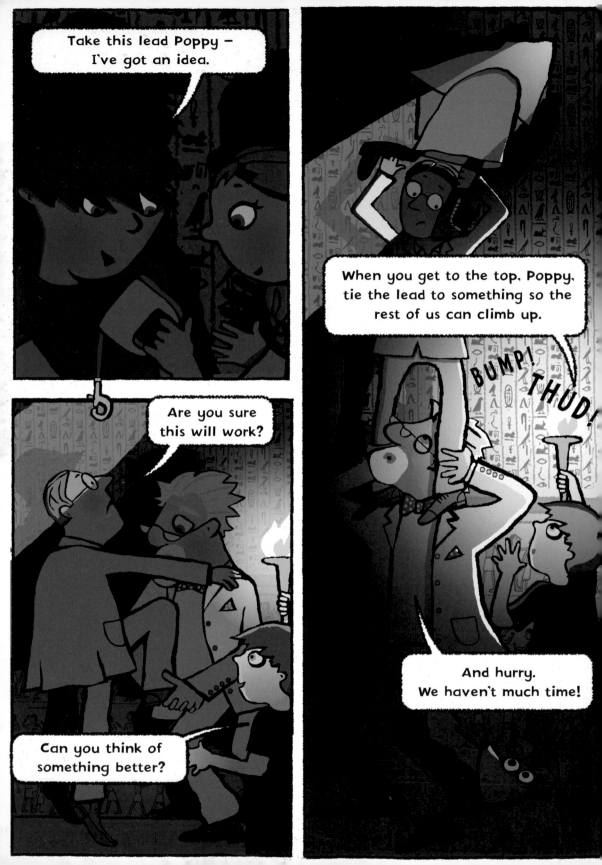

When I said I was happy to hang out with you guys, this is not what I had in mind.

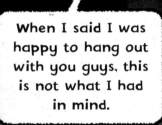

Yes! Thank you. The Pharaoh wishes to see you now. But perhaps a change of attire is in order first?

Her Majesty... er, I mean Her Eminence... No, that's not quite right either...

The Pharaoh?

THE NEXT DAY...

What are you doing?

Walking like an Egyptian. What else?

We're finally going to discover the Eye of Pakhet and all you two can do is lark about!

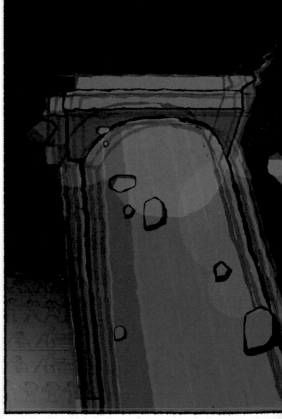

Good boy, Bandit!

I say, well done Poppy!

You rock!

I what?

Now we just have to work out how to use this Eye of Pakhet thingy.

I've got a better idea. Poppy, you tie up those two. Jack, help me with this will you?

Renowned archaeologist Dr Jack Honeycut started his distinguished career as a boy, assisting his grandfather, the respected Professor Winston Honeycut. Together their work and discoveries have advanced considerably our understanding of daily life in ancient Egypt.

Looks as if we'd better hurry up!

Amazing... way to go, Poppy!

The Eye of Pakhet, It's in us all, Bandit. It's in us all.

# Charlie's

## NOTEBOOK

Useful things to remember
if you're ever in
ancient Egypt.

Look at Jack, properly grown up with a weird hat!

# EGYPTOLOGY & ARCHAEOLOGY

Jack told me (in his long-winded way!) that Egyptology is the study of ancient Egypt – not just the history, but also the language they spoke, the writing they left, their religion and their art.

Like Professor Honeycut, many Egyptologists are also archaeologists. Archaeology is the study of a society through the stuff that it leaves behind – sometimes literally their rubbish!

Jack and the Professor were working in the early twentieth century, but the first Egyptologists were the ancient Egyptians themselves! That was because the ancient Egyptian civilisation lasted over 3000 years.

# THE SUFFRAGETTES

While Poppy and Jack were in Egypt with their grandfather, their mother was back in England fighting for the right of women to vote for who governed their country.

Poppy told me her mum was a member of the Women's Social and Political Union, formed in 1905 and otherwise known as the Suffragettes. Members were prepared to go to jail for their cause, and some did by smashing windows or chaining themselves to railings.

One woman, Emily Davidson, even died for her beliefs when she rushed onto the track at the Derby racecourse in an attempt to stop the king's horse!

At the museum, I read that women over the age of 30 got the right to vote in 1918, but the Suffragettes didn't stop their work until all adults over the age of 21 got the right to vote in 1928 – way to go Poppy!

Poppy's mum looks really proud of her loud daughter!

# A LAND OF HIDDEN TREASURES

Professor Honeycut told me that, for almost two thousand years, everyone more or less forgot about the amazing culture of ancient Egypt – sometimes it was literally buried! But in 1798, French explorers, led by their famous leader Napoleon Bonaparte, invaded Egypt. They brought scholars who wanted to study Egypt's history, and set up the Institute of Egypt outside of Cairo.

When I landed in Egypt in 1906, the Professor's main competition was a man called Howard Carter. Not only had Carter discovered the tomb of Hatshepsut in 1900, but he went on to discover many more, including the famous tomb of Tutankhamun (also known as King Tut) in 1922.

## TOMB RAIDERS

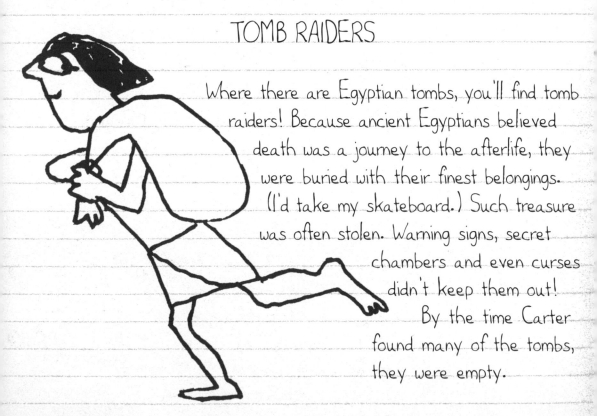

Where there are Egyptian tombs, you'll find tomb raiders! Because ancient Egyptians believed death was a journey to the afterlife, they were buried with their finest belongings. (I'd take my skateboard.) Such treasure was often stolen. Warning signs, secret chambers and even curses didn't keep them out! By the time Carter found many of the tombs, they were empty.

# THE PHARAOHS

The Pharaohs were the kings of ancient Egypt (even the women!). They were also considered gods by their followers and expected to carry out certain duties like making the sun rise and making sure the River Nile flooded each summer — talk about pressure on the job!

Pharaohs are separated into different ruling families or dynasties (no, not the TV show from the 1980s). During the ancient Egyptian civilisation, there were 30 dynasties. Some lasted for lots of pharaohs, some for just one. Hatshepsut reigned as the 5th pharaoh of the 18th dynasty, from about 1500 to 1460 BC.

# GODS, GODDESSES AND ANIMALS

The ancient Egyptians had loads (and loads!) of gods and goddesses. They thought some animals were sacred because they stood for a god or goddess — now that's what I call a society of animal lovers! Bastet and Sehkmet (the two goddesses that formed Pakhet) were shown as a cat and a lioness, the god Osiris was shown as a falcon and Thoth was a baboon!

Dogs were used for hunting and kept as pets in ancient Egypt. They weren't as popular as cats, but Anubis, god of the Underworld, did take the form of a jackal. The ancient Egyptian word for dog was 'iwiw' which referred to a dog's bark. I prefer 'Bandit'.

Bandit's Egyptian look!

# PHARAOH FASHION

On the whole, ancient Egyptians wore very few
clothes. It was so warm they didn't have to!
Children and the very poor often
wore nothing but their smiles!

Pharaoh-spotting must have been
pretty easy. The main piece of a
pharaoh's wardrobe was the
shendyt, which was like a
pleated apron, worn under
robes made from very
sheer linen. The headpieces
they wore were called nemes
and made of linen too. They also liked
to wear decorated sandals, loads of jewellery, and khol around the eyes –
sounds like Mum on holiday!

## FAKE BEARDS

Pharaohs were considered kings even if, like Hatshepsut, they were
actually women. As the pharaoh was considered the
son of the chief Egyptian god, Ra, he had to be
a man or at least look like one. What's a girl to
do? Wear a chin wig, of course! Hatshepsut
added to her manly look by often
wearing men's clothes too.

# BENI HASAN AND
# THE TEMPLE OF PAKHET

When you travel back in time, it's always good to have a map. Luckily Jack had plenty, so we always knew where we were. Beni Hasan is an ancient Egyptian burial site in Middle Egypt. It's between the ancient capitals of Asyut and Memphis (not the one in Tennessee). According to Professor Honeycut, most of the building happened in the Middle Kingdom, from the 21st to 17th centuries BC. Almost all of the 39 tombs were built straight into the rock cliffs. The more important a person was, the higher up the cliffs he was buried.

The temple of Pakhet, started by Hatshepsut and later finished by Thutmose III, is about a mile south of Beni Hasan. Most of the temple was built underground and is covered in decorations.

# THE RIVER NILE

The River Nile was essential to the Egyptians - it was not only the motorway of the ancient world, but also provided rich soil for crops and helped to discourage pesky neighbours from invading. For years the Nile flooded at almost the exact same time. In fact the Egyptian year was divided into three seasons based on the River Nile: flood season, planting season and harvest season.

Most ancient Egyptian tombs were built on the western side of the Nile, but the tombs I went into at Beni Hasan were built into the rock cliffs on the Eastern side of the river.

# HIEROGLYPHS & THE ROSETTA STONE

My handwriting has never been great, so I can only imagine how tough it must have been to write in hieroglyphs. Known as 'the words of the gods', hieroglyphs were first used by priests. Written in rows or columns, they can be read from left to right or from right to left. Sounds confusing, but it's not really. You can tell the direction in which the text is meant to be read by looking at the direction in which the animal or human figures are facing. The figures always face towards the beginning of the line.

For thousands of years no one could remember how to translate ancient Egyptian, but in 1799 a French soldier discovered a large stone slab in Egypt. Known as the Rosetta Stone, it had the same message carved into it in three languages: hieroglyphs at the top, demotic script (which ancient Egyptians developed after hieroglyphs) in the middle, and ancient Greek at the bottom.

It turned out that this stone was a proclamation by a Greek ruler called Ptolemy V — he had to write it in three languages, so that everyone in his empire could understand what he was on about.

In 1822, another Frenchman named Jean-François Champollion used the stone and his knowledge of Greek to translate the meaning of the hieroglyphs. Think I'll stick with the ABCs!

This is 'Bandit', spelt in hieroglyphs!

# MUMMIES

After all the trouble they caused, Dr Bull and Haru were sent to the embalming priests to help them turn rich (dead) Egyptians into mummies. Mummification was important to the Egyptians – they believed that, when the world ended, they would need their earthly bodies to travel to the afterlife. If their bodies had rotted, they wouldn't be able to go.

Unfortunately for the embalming priests, bodies rotted quickly in the Egyptian heat. So they followed a little recipe: take one dead Egyptian, chuck clothing, then carefully remove brain with iron hook shoved up the nostril. (Won't be using that in the afterlife!) Fill head with a mix of plaster and a salty chemical called natron. Take out all organs except the heart and put them in canopic jars filled with natron, then seal. Stuff torso with rags and a selection of spices then sew back up. Soak body in natron for 70 days, then wrap in bandages and decorate with head mask, charms and written prayers as desired. Put in coffin and serve up at funeral ceremony, before shutting in tomb for some lucky Egyptologist to find!